ACCELERATE PRODUCTIVITY 1:3:5 PLANNER

PENNY ZENKER

P10 Productivity Accelerator

INTRODUCTION

Staying focused on your goals requires constant focus on the goals and activities that help you reach your goals. This means planning and scheduling daily with conscious thought and attention to what tasks will move you forward on long term goals, milestones and daily urgencies.

Action is good but without planning, action can be wasted. Focused action happens when goals and actions are aligned.

The 1:3:5 Daily planning method help you to align tasks and goals and maintain a balance between urgent and important.

1 Long Term Strategic Action

3 Milestone Driven Actions

5 Urgent Tasks (that must get done by you today)

An important part of any planning g process is reflecting and adapting. This daily planning method allows for reflection at the end of every day and every week to reflect on what worked and what didn't work so you can be flexible in how you approach your time and priorities.

If you want further support in reaching your goals faster go to www.p10app.com and look at other tools and resources, blogs, and coaching opportunities.

Be Productive!

Penny

Plan Milestones and key deliverables. What's the Month Theme?

Month Year MARCH 2019

Sun	Mon	Tues	Wed	Thu	Fri	Satur	
3	4	5	6	7	8	9	WEEK 1
10	11	12	13	14	15	16	WEEK 2
17	18	19	20	21	22	23	WEEK 3
24	25	26	27	28	29	30	WEEK 4

Notes:

1) Biz Plan
2) Exec Summary
3) Follow-up Shima seki NJ
4) " Steve

(P)
* Costs down
* Secure supply

(M)
* Create Etsy account

Date: 3 / 4 / 19

1:3:5 Daily Planning »»

1 LT Strategic Goal

① Costs down
② secure supply

3 Important Milestones

1. _____
2. _____
3. _____

5 Must Do Today

1. Email Nancy Boss Babe
2. Create Etsy account
3. FP Red Antler
4. _____
5. _____

Intention

Daily Wins
- _____
- _____
- _____
- _____

Distractions
- _____
- _____
- _____
- _____

Gratitudes

NOTES

P10
www.p10app.com

Date: ___ / ___ / ___

1:3:5 Daily Planning »»

1 LT Strategic Goal

Intention

3 Important Milestones

Daily Wins
- ○ _____
- ○ _____
- ○ _____
- ○ _____

1. _____
2. _____
3. _____

5 Must Do Today

Distractions
- ○ _____
- ○ _____
- ○ _____
- ○ _____

1. _____
2. _____
3. _____
4. _____
5. _____

Gratitudes

⋯ **NOTES** ⋯

P10
www.p10app.com

Date: ___/___/___

1:3:5 Daily Planning »»

1 LT Strategic Goal

3 Important Milestones

1. _____
2. _____
3. _____

5 Must Do Today

1. _____
2. _____
3. _____
4. _____
5. _____

Intention

Daily Wins
- _____
- _____
- _____
- _____

Distractions
- _____
- _____
- _____
- _____

Gratitudes

NOTES

P10
www.p10app.com

Date: ___ / ___ / ___

1:3:5 Daily Planning »»

1 LT Strategic Goal

Intention

3 Important Milestones

Daily Wins

- ___
- ___
- ___
- ___

1. ___
2. ___
3. ___

Distractions

- ___
- ___
- ___
- ___

5 Must Do Today

1. ___
2. ___
3. ___
4. ___
5. ___

Gratitudes

⋯ NOTES ⋯

P10
www.p10app.com

Date: ___ / ___ / ___

1:3:5 Daily Planning »»

1 LT Strategic Goal

3 Important Milestones

1. _____
2. _____
3. _____

5 Must Do Today

1. _____
2. _____
3. _____
4. _____
5. _____

Intention

Daily Wins
- _____
- _____
- _____
- _____

Distractions
- _____
- _____
- _____
- _____

Gratitudes

NOTES

P10
www.p10app.com

Date: ___ / ___ / ___

1:3:5 Daily Planning ≫≫

1 LT Strategic Goal

_____
_____
_____

3 Important Milestones

1. _____
2. _____
3. _____

5 Must Do Today

1. _____
2. _____
3. _____
4. _____
5. _____

Intention

_____
_____
_____
_____

Daily Wins

○ _____
○ _____
○ _____
○ _____

Distractions

○ _____
○ _____
○ _____
○ _____

Gratitudes

_____
_____
_____
_____

NOTES

_____
_____
_____

P10
www.p10app.com

Date: ___ / ___ / ___

1:3:5 Daily Planning ▶▶

1 LT Strategic Goal

3 Important Milestones

1. _____
2. _____
3. _____

5 Must Do Today

1. _____
2. _____
3. _____
4. _____
5. _____

Intention

Daily Wins
- _____
- _____
- _____
- _____

Distractions
- _____
- _____
- _____
- _____

Gratitudes

NOTES

P10
www.p10app.com

"

CONNECTION CREATES CONVICTION

PENNY ZENKER

AUTHOR OF THE PRODUCTIVITY ZONE:
LEARN THE 10 CORE DRIVERS OF PRODUCTIVITY

"

Date: ___/___/___

1:3:5 Daily Planning »

1 LT Strategic Goal

3 Important Milestones

1. _____
2. _____
3. _____

5 Must Do Today

1. _____
2. _____
3. _____
4. _____
5. _____

Intention

Daily Wins
○ _____
○ _____
○ _____
○ _____

Distractions
○ _____
○ _____
○ _____
○ _____

Gratitudes

NOTES

P10
www.p10app.com

Date: ___/___/___

1:3:5 Daily Planning ▶▶

1 LT Strategic Goal

3 Important Milestones

1. _____
2. _____
3. _____

5 Must Do Today

1. _____
2. _____
3. _____
4. _____
5. _____

Intention

Daily Wins
- ○ _____
- ○ _____
- ○ _____
- ○ _____

Distractions
- ○ _____
- ○ _____
- ○ _____
- ○ _____

Gratitudes

NOTES

P10
www.p10app.com

Date: ___ / ___ / ___

**1:3:5
Daily Planning** »»

1 LT Strategic Goal

_____
_____
_____

3 Important Milestones

1. _____
2. _____
3. _____

5 Must Do Today

1. _____
2. _____
3. _____
4. _____
5. _____

Intention
_____
_____
_____
_____

Daily Wins
○ _____
○ _____
○ _____
○ _____

Distractions
○ _____
○ _____
○ _____
○ _____

Gratitudes
_____
_____
_____
_____

NOTES
_____
_____
_____

P10
www.p10app.com

Date: ___ / ___ / ___

1:3:5 Daily Planning »

1 LT Strategic Goal

3 Important Milestones

1. _____
2. _____
3. _____

5 Must Do Today

1. _____
2. _____
3. _____
4. _____
5. _____

Intention

Daily Wins
- o _____
- o _____
- o _____
- o _____

Distractions
- o _____
- o _____
- o _____
- o _____

Gratitudes

NOTES

P10
www.p10app.com

Date: ___ / ___ / ___

1:3:5 Daily Planning »»

1 LT Strategic Goal

3 Important Milestones

1.
2.
3.

5 Must Do Today

1.
2.
3.
4.
5.

Intention

Daily Wins
- ○
- ○
- ○
- ○

Distractions
- ○
- ○
- ○
- ○

Gratitudes

NOTES

www.p10app.com

Date: ___ / ___ / ___

1:3:5 Daily Planning »»»

1 LT Strategic Goal

3 Important Milestones

1. _____
2. _____
3. _____

5 Must Do Today

1. _____
2. _____
3. _____
4. _____
5. _____

Intention

Daily Wins
- _____
- _____
- _____
- _____

Distractions
- _____
- _____
- _____
- _____

Gratitudes

NOTES

P10
www.p10app.com

Date: ___ / ___ / ___

1:3:5 Daily Planning

1 LT Strategic Goal

Intention

3 Important Milestones

Daily Wins
- ○ _____
- ○ _____
- ○ _____
- ○ _____

1. _____
2. _____
3. _____

5 Must Do Today

Distractions
- ○ _____
- ○ _____
- ○ _____
- ○ _____

1. _____
2. _____
3. _____
4. _____
5. _____

Gratitudes

NOTES

P10
www.p10app.com

WORKING HARDER ONLY NARROWS PERSPECTIVE

PENNY ZENKER

AUTHOR OF THE PRODUCTIVITY ZONE:
LEARN THE 10 CORE DRIVERS OF PRODUCTIVITY

Date: ___ / ___ / ___

1:3:5 Daily Planning >>

Intention

1 LT Strategic Goal

_____

Daily Wins

- ○ _____
- ○ _____
- ○ _____
- ○ _____

3 Important Milestones

1. _____
2. _____
3. _____

Distractions

- ○ _____
- ○ _____
- ○ _____
- ○ _____

5 Must Do Today

1. _____
2. _____
3. _____
4. _____
5. _____

Gratitudes

NOTES

www.p10app.com

Date: ___ / ___ / ___

1:3:5 Daily Planning ≫

Intention

1 LT Strategic Goal

Daily Wins
- ○ _____
- ○ _____
- ○ _____
- ○ _____

3 Important Milestones

1. _____
2. _____
3. _____

Distractions
- ○ _____
- ○ _____
- ○ _____
- ○ _____

5 Must Do Today

1. _____
2. _____
3. _____
4. _____
5. _____

Gratitudes

NOTES

P10
www.p10app.com

Date: ___ / ___ / ___

1:3:5 Daily Planning ≫

1 LT Strategic Goal

Intention

_____
_____
_____
_____

3 Important Milestones

Daily Wins
○ _____
○ _____
○ _____
○ _____

1. _____
2. _____
3. _____

5 Must Do Today

Distractions
○ _____
○ _____
○ _____
○ _____

1. _____
2. _____
3. _____
4. _____
5. _____

Gratitudes

_____
_____
_____
_____

NOTES

_____
_____
_____

P10
www.p10app.com

Date: ___ / ___ / ___

| 1:3:5 Daily Planning >>> | Intention |

1 LT Strategic Goal

_____
_____
_____
_____

3 Important Milestones

1. _____
2. _____
3. _____

5 Must Do Today

1. _____
2. _____
3. _____
4. _____
5. _____

Intention

Daily Wins
- o _____
- o _____
- o _____
- o _____

Distractions
- o _____
- o _____
- o _____
- o _____

Gratitudes

NOTES
_____
_____
_____

P10
www.p10app.com

Date: ___ / ___ / ___

1:3:5 Daily Planning ▶▶

1 LT Strategic Goal

3 Important Milestones

1. _____
2. _____
3. _____

5 Must Do Today

1. _____
2. _____
3. _____
4. _____
5. _____

Intention

Daily Wins
- ○ _____
- ○ _____
- ○ _____
- ○ _____

Distractions
- ○ _____
- ○ _____
- ○ _____
- ○ _____

Gratitudes

NOTES

P10
www.p10app.com

Date: ___ / ___ / ___

1:3:5 Daily Planning ▶▶

1 LT Strategic Goal

Intention

3 Important Milestones

Daily Wins
- ○ _____
- ○ _____
- ○ _____
- ○ _____

1. _____
2. _____
3. _____

5 Must Do Today

Distractions
- ○ _____
- ○ _____
- ○ _____
- ○ _____

1. _____
2. _____
3. _____
4. _____
5. _____

Gratitudes

NOTES

P10
www.p10app.com

Date: ___ / ___ / ___

1:3:5 Daily Planning >>

Intention

1 | LT Strategic Goal

Daily Wins
- ○ _____
- ○ _____
- ○ _____
- ○ _____

3 | Important Milestones

1. _____
2. _____
3. _____

Distractions
- ○ _____
- ○ _____
- ○ _____
- ○ _____

5 | Must Do Today

1. _____
2. _____
3. _____
4. _____
5. _____

Gratitudes

NOTES

P10
www.p10app.com

TRY TO CONTROL SOMETHING AND IT CONTROLS YOU

PENNY ZENKER

AUTHOR OF THE PRODUCTIVITY ZONE:
LEARN THE 10 CORE DRIVERS OF PRODUCTIVITY

Date: ___ / ___ / ___

1:3:5 Daily Planning >>>

1 LT Strategic Goal

3 Important Milestones

1. _____
2. _____
3. _____

5 Must Do Today

1. _____
2. _____
3. _____
4. _____
5. _____

Intention

Daily Wins
- _____
- _____
- _____
- _____

Distractions
- _____
- _____
- _____
- _____

Gratitudes

NOTES

P10
www.p10app.com

Date: ___/___/___

1:3:5 Daily Planning ▶▶

1 LT Strategic Goal

Intention

3 Important Milestones

Daily Wins
- ○
- ○
- ○
- ○

1.
2.
3.

5 Must Do Today

Distractions
- ○
- ○
- ○
- ○

1.
2.
3.
4.
5.

Gratitudes

NOTES

P10
www.p10app.com

Date: ___ / ___ / ___

1:3:5 Daily Planning

1 LT Strategic Goal

Intention

3 Important Milestones

Daily Wins

1. ___
2. ___
3. ___

5 Must Do Today

Distractions

1. ___
2. ___
3. ___
4. ___
5. ___

Gratitudes

NOTES

P10
www.p10app.com

Date: ___ / ___ / ___

1:3:5 Daily Planning >>

Intention

1 LT Strategic Goal

Daily Wins

- ○ _____
- ○ _____
- ○ _____
- ○ _____

3 Important Milestones

1. _____
2. _____
3. _____

Distractions

- ○ _____
- ○ _____
- ○ _____
- ○ _____

5 Must Do Today

1. _____
2. _____
3. _____
4. _____
5. _____

Gratitudes

NOTES

P10
www.p10app.com

Date: ___/___/___

1:3:5 Daily Planning

1 LT Strategic Goal

___

3 Important Milestones

1. ___
2. ___
3. ___

5 Must Do Today

1. ___
2. ___
3. ___
4. ___
5. ___

Intention

___

Daily Wins

- ___
- ___
- ___
- ___

Distractions

- ___
- ___
- ___
- ___

Gratitudes

___

NOTES

___

P10
www.p10app.com

Date: ___ / ___ / ___

1:3:5 Daily Planning

1 LT Strategic Goal

3 Important Milestones

1. _____
2. _____
3. _____

5 Must Do Today

1. _____
2. _____
3. _____
4. _____
5. _____

Intention

Daily Wins

- _____
- _____
- _____
- _____

Distractions

- _____
- _____
- _____
- _____

Gratitudes

NOTES

P10
www.p10app.com

Date: ___ / ___ / ___

1:3:5 Daily Planning »»

1 LT Strategic Goal

3 Important Milestones

1. _____
2. _____
3. _____

5 Must Do Today

1. _____
2. _____
3. _____
4. _____
5. _____

Intention

Daily Wins
- o _____
- o _____
- o _____
- o _____

Distractions
- o _____
- o _____
- o _____
- o _____

Gratitudes

NOTES

P10
www.p10app.com

"

BE THE ENERGY YOU WANT TO SEE IN OTHERS

PENNY ZENKER

AUTHOR OF THE PRODUCTIVITY ZONE
LEARN THE 10 CORE DRIVERS OF PRODUCTIVITY

"

TRACKING:

Monthly Goal Progress Chart

Goal	

For each day, put a dot at your percent. Connect the dots to track your results.

Day	10%	20%	30%	40%	50%	60%	70%	80%	90%	100%
31										
30										
29										
28										
27										
26										
25										
24										
23										
22										
21										
20										
19										
18										
17										
16										
15										
14										
13										
12										
11										
10										
9										
8										
7										
6										
5										
4										
3										
2										
1										

Monthly Goal Progress Chart

Goal

For each day, put a dot at your percent. Connect the dots to track your results.

Day	10%	20%	30%	40%	50%	60%	70%	80%	90%	100%
31										
30										
29										
28										
27										
26										
25										
24										
23										
22										
21										
20										
19										
18										
17										
16										
15										
14										
13										
12										
11										
10										
9										
8										
7										
6										
5										
4										
3										
2										
1										

Monthly Goal Progress Chart

Goal	

For each day, put a dot at your percent. Connect the dots to track your results.

Day	10%	20%	30%	40%	50%	60%	70%	80%	90%	100%
31										
30										
29										
28										
27										
26										
25										
24										
23										
22										
21										
20										
19										
18										
17										
16										
15										
14										
13										
12										
11										
10										
9										
8										
7										
6										
5										
4										
3										
2										
1										

Monthly Goal Progress Chart

Goal

For each day, put a dot at your percent. Connect the dots to track your results.

Day	10%	20%	30%	40%	50%	60%	70%	80%	90%	100%
31										
30										
29										
28										
27										
26										
25										
24										
23										
22										
21										
20										
19										
18										
17										
16										
15										
14										
13										
12										
11										
10										
9										
8										
7										
6										
5										
4										
3										
2										
1										

Made in the USA
Middletown, DE
14 February 2019